ISBN 978-1-331-70245-0
PIBN 10223527

This book is a reproduction of an important historical work. Forgotten Books uses
state-of-the-art technology to digitally reconstruct the work, preserving the original format
whilst repairing imperfections present in the aged copy. In rare cases, an imperfection in
the original, such as a blemish or missing page, may be replicated in our edition. We do,
however, repair the vast majority of imperfections successfully; any imperfections that
remain are intentionally left to preserve the state of such historical works.

# 1 MONTH OF
# FREE
# READING

## at

## www.ForgottenBooks.com

By purchasing this book you are eligible for one month membership to ForgottenBooks.com, giving you unlimited access to our entire collection of over 1,000,000 titles via our web site and mobile apps.

To claim your free month visit:
www.forgottenbooks.com/free223527

English
Français
Deutsche
Italiano
Español
Português

# www.forgottenbooks.com

**Mythology** Photography **Fiction**
Fishing Christianity **Art** Cooking
Essays Buddhism Freemasonry
Medicine **Biology** Music **Ancient
Egypt** Evolution Carpentry Physics
Dance Geology **Mathematics** Fitness
Shakespeare **Folklore** Yoga Marketing
**Confidence** Immortality Biographies
Poetry **Psychology** Witchcraft
Electronics Chemistry History **Law**
Accounting **Philosophy** Anthropology
Alchemy Drama Quantum Mechanics
Atheism Sexual Health **Ancient History**
**Entrepreneurship** Languages Sport
Paleontology Needlework Islam
**Metaphysics** Investment Archaeology
Parenting Statistics Criminology
**Motivational**

A number of the poems in this volume are here included through the courtesy of the publishers of the Century Magazine, Harper's Monthly, Scribner's Magazine, The Bellman, the London Bookman, the Nation, the Ladies' Home Journal, Lippincott's, Harper's Bazaar, the De-lineator, and the Poetry Journal, in which magazines they first appeared.

# CONTENTS

## CONTENTS

# CONTENTS

# DEEP PLACES

# JEHANE

"And had she come so far for this —
"To part at last without a kiss,
"Beside the haystack in the floods!"

*Morris.*

IN garments gray of sleety rain
  The wind across the sodden plain
Went visibly, and through it went
Gray as a gust, her slender form
Swathed in wet robes, and forward bent
Against the pushing of the storm.
Stumbling she ran, as one far spent,
But the pale splendour of her face
Was set as toward a trysting place,
And there was need of glances twain
Ere one could see the lines of pain
Round lips grown patient ere their day,
And mark the early white that lay
Like Lenten ashes in her hair.
She went with eyes that never swerved
Until at last she halted where
The glazing pools had wellnigh drowned
A heap of timbers that had served
To prop a haystack, in years past.
She stretched her on the icy ground

[ 1 ]

JEHANE (continued)

*Sighing for sheer content, as one*
*Who wearied leans when day is done*
*Upon love's breast, and said —*

                    At last —
At last I come to you, to tell
Of all these years.  If ill or well
I did, judge you; and yet, somehow,
I think you will not judge me, now,
But only stoop from God's right hand
And whisper, "Dear, I understand."
Can they have wiped in Paradise
So well the sorrow from your eyes
That from your heart is cleansed away
Even the shadow of that day
When you and I, in just this place,
Met death and Godmar face to face
Beside the haystack in the floods?
You by the sword to perish, I
Later by bitter ways to die
In Paris as a sorceress
Unless . . . but there was no "unless"
For me, who loved you so, I knew
At such a price, each breath you drew

JEHANE (continued)

Would strangle you. I answered No.
I never have forgot to miss
Through all these years, the single kiss
Denied our parting, long ago.
But then I saw the end so near
I thought, "Not long the waiting, Dear,
"Until we meet!" . . . I did not know. . . .

WHEN you were dead, he freed from stain
His blade, and sheathed it. Through
the rain
We rode toward Paris. Wet and gray
Closed in the curtains of the day,
And as we rode, I thought,—"To night!
"Death is a bridal flower of white,
"Mine for the plucking!" And I swore
That you and I should meet before
The mockery of another dawn.
Rapt from the flesh I rode, and ere
I woke to know that we had drawn
Rein at an inn, Godmar was there
Beside my stirrup. Down I slid
Ere he could touch me.

JEHANE (continued)

                       " What I did,
" You bade me do! "  I heard his breath
Catch like a sob.  " You still choose death,
" Jehane?  It is not yet too late —"
It seemed I was too tired to hate,
For I felt nothing.  Pale and grim
I saw the tortured face of him
An evil star against the night,
And then — it faded. . . .
                      When the sight
Came back to me, I lay in bed,
An old bent woman o'er my head
Crooning in mother-wise, her face
Kind in the firelight.  " Mary's grace
" Be praised," she cried, " you live at length!
" Drink   this,   dear   lady,   mend   your
      strength! "
I turned away, but —   " Think! " she said;
" A double hunger must be fed.
" Not yours alone the need."
                       My heart
Stopped.  Then it strove to beat apart
My breast.  With lips grown stiff and cold

JEHANE (continued)

I stammered, " He must not be told —
" Godmar — as you may hope for Heaven! "
" No whisper, by the Sorrows Seven! "
She vowed, and then — " You had not
    known?
" Poor child. . . ."
                I might have been her own.
I cannot pray for her by name —
God knows her, though.
                The morning came,
But now I could not bear to die.
The trees against a perfect sky
Prickled with twigs.  It seemed that I
Was part of the awakening earth
And that to bring your child to birth
Was all for which myself was made.
I would have trodden unafraid
Hell's deepest, with that end in sight.
Robert — the gates of hell that night
Again stood open.  I went in. . . .

JEHANE (continued)

I CARED as little for the sin
   As for the anguish and the shame.
It seemed my secret swept like flame
Body and soul, and burned them clean.
About his castle, gold and green
The thickets kindled, and I said
Within my heart, " When they grow red. . . .
God pitied me; ere spring was spent
War called to Godmar, and he went.
Watched like a prisoner was I
But strangely sweet the days went by
Until I smiled to see at last
The crimson leaves come whirling past.
Robert — the rapture of that pain!

WHEN with the snows he came again,
   I had resolved what must be done.
Silent I met him, with my son
Held in my arms.  He stopped astound.
In all the room there was no sound
But his hoarse breathing.  Then —
                        " Jehane . . . .
" I had not thought of — this . . ." he said.

JEHANE (continued)

WITH solemn masses we were wed.
    What mattered it that Godmar gave
The boy his name?  There were your
    brave
Clear eyes — your brow —
                    I feared to bear
Godmar a child, lest he compare
The twain, when he must needs have
    known. . . .
But years went by, with yours alone
The pivot of our household pride.
He seemed the gallant heart that died
In me, with you.  And Godmar — strange
That simple happiness can change
A man so much!  Thwarted desire
Made him a fiend — but when the fire
Was left unchecked, it swiftly burned
Its violence away, and turned
To comfortable embers, fit
To warm a hearth where musing sit
Good placid folk whose youth is done.
While he would talk of what " our son "
Should do, sometime — far far away

JEHANE (continued)

As through the rain, I saw that day
When murdered at his feet you lay,
And thought, could it be I and he
Who sat at meat so quietly,
Your boy between us!
                        Years that seem,
Now they are over, like a dream
I am too weary to recall. . . .
The night he died, I told him all.
One heavy tear slid down his cheek.
He fought for breath awhile, then, weak
But clear, he spoke — "My heir . . . the
        same. . . ."
No more.  And so to Godmar came
His touch of greatness at the end.
I prayed for him as for a friend.

ROBERT, it seems to me to-day
        No life is wholly thrown away.
We are the seedcorn, you and I,
Dead in the dark, that youth may pry
The clods asunder toward the sky.
My part is played, my task is done.

JEHANE (continued)

Life opens nobly to our son.
The King has made him knight, and he
Has now no longer need of me —
Man as he is, and true, and strong. . . .
The kiss that I have kept so long,—
It seems that all my life has passed
Into that kiss . . . and now . . . at last,
Beloved . . . now. . . .

     *A sigh, and then*
*No other sound.  So still she lay*
*The hailstones on her mantle gray*
*Deepened to little drifts like snow.*
*This was the way they met again*
*Where they had parted, long ago.*

## ALLAH IS WITH THE PATIENT

ALLAH is with the patient. Long ago
    I sat with eyes and thoughts that wan-
    dered far
And heard as in a dream my father's voice
Speaking to me as now I speak to thee,
Who heedest little as I heeded him.
What place had patience in a young man's
    heart?
The sky was languid with the sunset glow,
The sweet air swooned with purple mys-
    teries,—
Was it an hour for aught but eagerness
As women passed on slender tinkling feet,
Flashing like jewelled beetles from the dusk,
And vanishing again, yet leaving clear
A trail of perfume on the evening air
That drew a man to follow? Who was I
To squat with gray-beards by the waning
    fire?

ALLAH IS WITH THE PATIENT (continued)

Well I remember how the challenge came
Of jasmine scent from wayward garments
    blown
And how I leapt to meet it!  As I went,
I heard my father sighing in his beard,
"Allah  is  with  the  patient."  But  there
    comes
An end to eagerness.  I had not thought
I could grow weary of enkindling eyes,
Slight  luring  limbs,  and  fingers  trained  to
    beat
The song of passion on the hearts of men
As on a darabukkeh.  But there came
A night when I grew sick of jasmine scent
As of the scent of fever, and the sight
Of smiling lips moist-parted left me cold —
A night when walls closed like a trap on me,
And like a grave-stone lay upon my head
The shadow of the roof.  So I went out
Under the calm illimitable sky,
Under the quiet scrutiny of stars
That stood apart like spirits, and looked on,
And as I felt the sweep of desert wind

ALLAH IS WITH THE PATIENT (continued)

Upon my face, I raised my voice and sang.
" Wise with much seeing are the eyes of
 night.
" What can amaze, what sicken, what delight
" The passionless cold vigil of the stars?
" Too much has been for any more to be
" That can dismay their far tranquil-
 lity. . . ."


I DID not sing the ending of the song,
 " Thine eyes are like the stars, O heart of
  me —
" Like the unmoved omniscience of the
 stars. . . ."
I could not sing those words; the eyes I knew
Smouldered like perfumed braziers near to
 earth,
Or like the homely embers that make warm
The cooking-pot. " Perchance in Paradise,"
I thought, " the houris that are Allah's glance
" Of favour on the faithful, have those eyes
" Of wise and starry calm. I will await

## ALLAH IS WITH THE PATIENT (continued)

"The gaze of them." And as there came to
    me
A sudden memory of my father's words,
I flung them like a challenge to the stars —
"Allah is with the patient!" I was
    young. . . .


THE hand of power on our village closed,
    For there was war; and many of the
      youths
Went full of heaviness, with backward eyes.
It was not so with me; gladly I strode
As to a feast, and bright upon me shone
The lifted brows of peril — but I found
Small glory in that war; of hunger much,
And much of weariness and aching limbs,
Much of the lurking death we could not see
That trod our shadows, striking from be-
    hind —
The sudden bullet singing from the waste
Was our mean death-chant, not the gener-
    ous cry

## ALLAH IS WITH THE PATIENT (continued)

Of clanging steel; it seemed we never
    ceased
Panting across interminable sands
Down into troughs that, sneering, the mir-
    age
Painted with blue like sky-reflecting pools,
Up over ridges where the sand slid back,
Drowning the print the lifted foot had left,
Sweating we laboured; always as it seemed
We came too late for glory. Other swords
In hostile blood found easing of their thirst,
And other eyes with pride of battle
    burned,—
Not ours, that strained too often toward the
    blue
That mocked us in the hollows of the sand
Looked dull upon a pool that was no lie,
As when we knew that we were free to seek
Our homes again, and that the war was
    done
And victory was ours, that " victory "
Left us but listless, for its sound was flat
Like a cracked cymbal. Once again I said

## ALLAH IS WITH THE PATIENT (continued)

"Allah is with the patient!" and a man
Who heard it, laughed.  His laugh was ill
    to hear,
But lo, his eyes gave back my face to me,
And my own smile was bitterer than his.
But softly spoke another, " Dost thou laugh,
" Brother?  It is no jest — the word is
    true —
" Allah is with the patient.  Blessed be
" His name to all the ages."  " It is well
" For thee to speak, perchance," the laugh-
    er said.
" Thou goest gladly to a waiting home;
" What dost thou care for glory?  But for
    me
" A woman waits who will but spit on me
" Since I have won no fame to honour her."
" And I," then cried myself, " for me there
    waits
" No woman anywhere; my only hope
" Was glory for the glory's sake, and now,
" Cheated of that, I am a dupe indeed."
" Nay," said our comrade gently, and I saw

## ALLAH IS WITH THE PATIENT (continued)

A little pulse that quivered in his cheek,
" For me there waits no woman.  She is
    dead,
" And on her breast the babe I never saw
" Is also dead.  I had no will to go —
" The soldiers took me.  Blessed be the
    name
" Of Allah —"  " And you still can say," I
    cried,
" That he is with the patient? "  Then he
    turned
The slow majestic sadness of his look
Full upon me.  " Were it not so," he said,
" Would they not be more lonely than the
    stars? "
He went away, and left us there afraid —
And yet he was a little man, and weak.
Humbler I turned me homeward, for I
    knew
There was a thing I had not understood.
When to the village I came back at last,
There were no songs for me.  I looked for
    none.

ALLAH IS WITH THE PATIENT (continued)

Only my father met me at the door
And peered into my face, for he was old
And saw but little — yet he saw enough
To make him smile. " It is my son," he
    said,
" He has come back to me a man at last —
" Allah is with the patient."
                       So I stayed
Quiet among my people, and I ploughed
My father's feddans, and the days went
    by.
I wedded and was faithful — if at times
Dreams drew me forth alone beneath the
    stars,
She found me no less kindly for the dreams.
Then thou wert born, and when I looked on
    thee
As full of pride she laid thee in my arms,
I saw in thee those wise and starry eyes
Of lonely glory — and my heart was glad,
Finding my dream come true. But with
    the years
The heavenly wonder died, and in its place

## ALLAH IS WITH THE PATIENT (continued)

The old earth-wonder came.  And then I
    thought
" Would he but learn of me —"  Ah! he is
    gone. . . .
Each for himself must turn the page of life
And read its wisdom through a blur of
    tears,
And yet — might I have made it clear to
    him,
My son!  May Allah, blessed be his name,
Allah, whose heart has yearned the ages
    through
To every generation, as my heart
Yearns to my son,— may Allah give him
    light.
Thou who art with the patient, lead him
    home
And give me of thy patience, while I wait.

## AT DENDERA

HERE in this narrow chamber, where one ray
    Quickens the jewel-coloured walls, I stand
Alone, a Queen, to speak to thee, a Queen.
I, Cleopatra, lift my face to meet
Thy silent face, Hathor, in this thy house,
Hither I came through fields of mellow
    green
Where prostrate peasants lifted peering eyes
To see the Great Queen's passing; labour
    fell
Stricken to silence at the sight of me.
Only the patient saqquias wailed on
As round and round the blindfold bullocks
    trod —
And yet I knew behind me they arose
Like trampled grain, and went about their
    toil,
Even as my courtiers when my shadow falls
No more upon them, turn them to their
    sport.

AT DENDERA (continued)

That world — what has that world to do
    with me?
Here in thy temple, here am I at home,
For thou and I are one at heart.   To thee
Hath ever been my longing, though at first
I knew it not.   Earth was too beautiful —
I could not see beyond — and all of me
That was of earth, cried out for earth's de-
    light.
I was athirst for life, and royally
I took what I deemed life — ay, like a Queen
I crushed the grapes of mortal joy and
    drank
The wine thereof, and still I was athirst.
Again I sought new vintage, and again,
While to my fingers clung the lees like blood.
Hathor, thou Merciless!   I give thee thanks,
Through all those drunken days I thirsted
    still!
And yet I was so slow to understand,
Nor knew that when on passion's very
    mouth
I trembled and grew cold, it was thy face

AT DENDERA (continued)

That came between, slaying the transient joy
With thine immortal breath; and so I fled
From lover unto lover, till at last
I knew that not in man was my desire
Nor in the fruit of man. I came to thee,
Hathor, at last, as now I come to thee.
It is enough that I am beautiful
For Beauty's sake — I ask not that men's
    eyes
Caress my loveliness, nor that a child
Should bear it like a banner down the years.
Enough for me that I myself have lived
And looked upon thy face of mystery,
Thou Gladness of the gods. . . . I am con-
    tent.
Have I not proved what earth-bound hearts
    call joy?
Love . . . what is love? Have I not known
    desire,—
Yea, have I not brought forth a son? And
    yet
My heart was still athirst. Thou knowest,
    thou,

AT DENDERA (continued)

Smiling that still wise smile of thine.  Thou
    too
Hast borne a Horus, yet we worship thee
Not babe at breast, like Isis, but alone,
Mateless, unconquerable,— there is not one
Of all the gods may dare to call thee his,
Mistress of whom thou wilt, but slave of
    none.
Therefore, since thou hast shown to me thy
    way,
Free as the desert wind, I lift to thee
My hands, and in them, Egypt.  Unto thee
Will I raise up a temple, fairer far
Than even this; to thee will I raise up
Myself in perfect beauty, perfect power,
My foot upon the weakness of mankind,
Spurning it while it lifts me.  Men shall see
Hathor in Cleopatra, and bow down
Smitten to worship that shall know no end,
Yea,  even  Rome!  Thou  seest . . . and
    shalt see. . . .

*AND nearing cloudlike o'er the lower blue,
Antony's galley swelled her amber sails.*

## AT ROMEO'S TOMB

A Y, gentle stranger, here lies Romeo.
    Thou art no Veronese . . . from Flor-
    ence? What,
Speak they of Romeo so far away?
Tell me, my son, what do they say of him?
" The king of lovers — and a noble heart
" Unwilling to brook life when love was
    gone —"
Are they not young who say it — mates of
    thine?
So many words that blossom fulsome sweet
Ripen to bitter fruit as men grow old —
I would not have you think of Romeo thus.
His death was noble? Nay — it was but
    young.
No friend of his? I was his nearest friend,
Even more privy to his inmost mind
Than was Mercutio's self, I dare to say,
And therefore I would have thee think of him

AT ROMEO'S TOMB (continued)

Thoughts that shall change only toward ten-
    derness
As the blood cools and slackens in its race
And less of life lies in a woman's hand.
Judge not my Romeo as a man is judged. . . .
Hadst thou but seen him when he came to
    me!
(He knew that I would shelter him, poor
    child,
Though he had laid a score of Tybalts cold)
We heard Verona roaring through the
    streets
Louder than floods in spring. The memory
After so long, is pitiful to tears —
His heart was fluttering like the candle-flame
Before the altar, on a windy day.
Romeo a man? No, no — he was a child,
A slender, scarcely-budded slip of spring,
The calyx-bursting promise of a rose
Flung to the foamy rage of Adige
And beaten down the rapids to its doom —
A blade untempered, broken ere its time
In the great battle — oh, a child, a child

AT ROMEO'S TOMB (continued)

> Caught in the millstones that grind up men's
>     hearts
> To be the bread of centuries unborn.
> Dreaming, he was enamoured of a dream,
> And from the drowsy wonder of his eyes
> Rubbed life like sleep away; so burst on him
> The blinding day of immortality. . . .
> On him, who was not yet awake to earth!
> How like a child astray he must have stared
> Upon the pitying angels!
>                        Juliet?
> Ay, call her woman if thou wilt, for she
> Can bear thy judgment; but for Romeo —
> Pray thou for him to-night as for a child.
> My name?   'Tis Laurence.
>               Peace to thee, my son.

## PETRUCHIO'S WIFE

AY, go your ways, my lord.  Look where he
    struts
And ruffles it along the sunny street!
His doublet's broken at the seam again —
I'll look to it when he comes home.  He's
    worse
Than any wanton youngling on his gear.
A gallant bearing — he is well worth ten
Of my fair sister's pretty mummer.  Bah!
Playing the schoolmaster to win a bride
He might have had by knocking at the door
And shaking a fat purse!  Petruchio
Measures more nearly to a man's degree;
Yet he is but a boy, an o'er-grown boy.
Was ever man so easily deceived?
What, did he think that he could master me
By wearying my body, starving it,
Shaming it with vile raiment?  Bless the
    fool!
And yet I swear I did not bless him then —

PETRUCHIO'S WIFE (continued)

I could have slain him rather; but I thought,
" Kate, thou art married; make the best of it.
" Thou hadst been wiser to lead apes in hell,
" But since thy cup of folly has been poured,
" Drink it off smiling.  He shall pay anon."
There at Bianca's feast, when he would show
His power so braggartly, I had well-nigh
Defied him to his face,— but I recalled
Hortensio's fine madam, and her taunt.
" What other way to sting so well," thought
    I,
" As show myself the model, her the
    shrew? "
Eh, did I sweetly play the pattern wife?
Ask of Petruchio's purse, where merrily
His fellow-bridegroom's golden forfeits
    clinked —
(Until he spent the better part of them
Upon a cap richer an hundredfold
Than that I spurned to please him!)  Am I
    tamed?
Thus much, perhaps . . . that now I play
    my part

PETRUCHIO'S WIFE (continued)

Not bitterly, but laughing in a sleeve
Which now is fashioned to my own desire,
I praying his approval; and instead
Of anger at his boastful boyishness
Is something, neither pity nor yet love —
The child of both, perchance.
                          I used to think
That when I held the larder keys, himself
Should fast some day, to pay that fast of
    mine.
But when the time came, I no longer cared
For little vengeance on a little wrong.
And so I feed him well, and speak him fair,
And keep him bravely clad, and when he
    meets
His friends, he vaunts the merits of his
    wife,
While they all marvel at the mastered
    shrew!
Look — he comes home — he's never long
    away.
How boyish-gay he waves an eager hand,
Seeing me waiting at the window here!

PETRUCHIO'S WIFE (continued)

God rest thee merry, good Petruchio;
How I could love thee . . . wert thou more
    a man!

*My excellent dear lord!   Art thou returned?*
*Then is the day grown bright for Katharine!*

# RAMESES WORSHIPS RAMESES AT ABU SIMBEL

OF all the gods I understand thee least,
    Thou god whose altar is the heart of me;
Therefore I leave the Others to the priest
While I myself do reverence to thee.
Avails my worship aught? The incense
    mounts
In silent exhalation like a prayer
Made visible — what sense of thine accounts
Acceptable its fragrance? Thou art —
    where?
I call unto the Others, and they hear;
But thou — I cannot tell. Thou art too
    near.

      \*      \*      \*      \*      \*

THE Sun I know: the lotus-bud of dawn
    Through countless vigils have I seen un-
      fold,
Veil after veil of green and rose withdrawn

## RAMESES WORSHIPS RAMESES (continued)

Yielding at last the blinding heart of gold
To me expectant.  I have known the Sun,
His kindness and his wrath, as I have known
The counsellor who sits at my right hand,
Yet thou to me art still the Hidden One.
The cold mysterious Moon, pacing alone
His jewelled house — the restless golden
    sand
Forever changing, like another sea —
The fruitful River in its majesty,
Mother alike and father of our land —
These I can see, these I can understand.
What veil impenetrable shelters Thee?
    *      *      *      *      *

THE Judges of the darkness and the dead,
    Unhuman arbiters of heaven and hell,
Creatures whose face is not the face of man,
Creatures whose power of life and death
    began
With life and death, and shall with them be
    sped —
Unseen, I know them; yea, I know them
    well.

RAMESES WORSHIPS RAMESES (continued)

I call them each by name . . . but thou
    Unknown,
What name have I to call thee save mine
    own?

   *       *       *       *       *

MINE own — and yet I know thou art not I.
    Here in this temple have I honoured thee
Where by the River, carven giant-high,
My fourfold image, eloquently dumb,
Sits dominating centuries to come.
I say it is thine Image — do I lie?

   *       *       *       *       *

ACROSS my proudest moments I have heard
    Thy terrible hushed laughter; stranger
    still —
Sometimes amid the battle, as I fought
With a god's fury, plain as spoken word
Thy patient weary sigh revealed to me
My rage as futile as the prize I sought.
And often when my courage has been chill
With inward questioning, my languor caught
Fire of a sudden from thy smile unseen.

## RAMESES WORSHIPS RAMESES (continued)

Again, when some flushed vision swift and
    keen
Struck music from my fancy, as the sun
From Memnon, came thy calm, unuttered
    scorn —
"So many lessons — dullard, still un-
    taught?"

    *        *        *        *        *

THOU art a god, and I am but a king.
    The people hail me god, and oft a glow
Responsive thrills me, till thy thought I
    know —
" Thou simple fool, thou perishable thing,
"'Tis I they worship — thou art but the
    shrine."
Nay, I am more — else could I know thee
    there?
I know that in some sort I am divine.
Yea, this I know — and yet I know not
    how —
When the last mystery to me is bare,
The underworld shall show me on thy brow
The final beauty Death has wrought on mine.

## IN THE ROMAN FORUM

NOTHING but beauty, now.
    No longer at the point of goading fear
The sullen, tributary world comes near
Before all-subjugating Rome to bow.
No more the pavement of the Forum rings
To breathless victory's exultant tread
Before the heavy march of captive kings.
Here stood the royal dead
In sculptured immortality, their gaze
Remote above the turmoil of the street
Hoarse with its living struggle at their feet.
Here spoke the law — that voice of bronze
    was heard
By all the world, and stirred
The latent mind of nations in the bud.
Bright with the laurels, bitter with the
    blood
Of heroes upon heroes was this place
Where the strong heart of an imperial race

IN THE ROMAN FORUM (continued)

Beat with the essence of a nation's life.
Princes and people evermore at strife —
Incense and worship — clash of armoured
    rage —
Ambition soaring up the sky like flame —
Interminable war that mortals wage
From century to century the same.
Still Fortune holds the crown for those who
    dare;
Mankind in many a distant otherwhere
Leaps panting toward the promise of her
    face —
But here, no more of coveting nor care.
No longer here the weltering human tide
Sluices the market-place and scatters wide
The weak as foam, to perish where they
    list.
Now by the sovereign Silence purified
Spring showers all with fragrant amethyst.
Were once these pulses violent and swift
As those that shake the cities of to-day?
How indolently sweet the petals drift
From yonder nodding spray!

IN THE ROMAN FORUM (continued)

Warming their broidered raiment in the sun
The little bright-eyed lizards bask and run
O'er fallen temples gracious in decay.
Man's arrogance with calculated art
Boasted in marble — now the quiet heart
Of the Great Mother dreams eternal things
In brief bright roses and ethereal green,
Or more exuberant, sings
In poppies poured profusely to the air
From secret hoards of scarlet. Nothing
     seen
But swoons with beauty — beauty every-
     where —
Nothing but beauty . . . now.
Here is the immortality of Rome.
Not where the city rises, dome on dome,
Seek we the living soul of ancient might,
But in this temple of green silence — here
Flame purer than the vestal is alight.
The world again draws near
In reverence, but now it comes to pay
The tribute of a nobler coin than fear.
In wondering worship, not in fierce dismay,

## IN THE ROMAN FORUM (continued)

Men bow the knee to what of Rome re-
    mains.
Time's long lustration has effaced her
    stains.
All that is perishable now is past
And earth her portion tenderly transmutes
To evanescent beauty of her own,
Jubilant flowers and nectar-breathing fruits,
Leaving in deathless glory at the last
Divinity alone.

## PERUGIA

FOR the sake of a weathered gray city set high
on a hill
To the northward I go,
Where Umbria's valley lies mile upon emer-
ald mile
Outspread like a chart.
The wind in her steep narrow streets is eter-
nally chill
From the neighbouring snow,
But linger who will in the lure of a southerly
smile,
Here is my heart.

WROUGHT to a mutual blueness are moun-
tains and sky;
Intermingling they meet.
Little gray breathings of olive arise from
the plain
Like sighs that are seen,

PERUGIA (continued)

> For man and his maker harmonious toil,
>     and the sigh
> Of such labour is sweet,
> And the fruits of their patience are vistas
>     of vineyards and grain
> In a glory of green.

NO wind from the valley that passes the
    casement but flings
Invisible flowers.
The carol of birds is a gossamer tissue of
    gold
On a background of bells.
Sweetest of all in the silence the nightingale
    sings
Through the silver-pure hours,
Till the stars disappear like a dream that
    may never be told,
That the dawning dispels.

PERUGIA (continued)

NEVER so darkling an alley but opens at last
On unlimited space,
Each gate is the frame of a vision that
stretches away
To the rims of the sky.
Never a scar that was left by the pitiless
past
But has taken a grace
Like the mark of a smile that was turned
upon children at play
In a summer gone by.

MANY the tyrants, my city, that held thee in
thrall.
What remains of them now?
Names whispered back from the dark
through a portal ajar —
They come not again.
By men thou wert made and wert marred,
but outlasting them all
Is the soul that is thou —
A soul that shall speak to my soul till I too
pass afar,
And perchance, even then.

## IN BOZEN OF A SUNDAY

IN Bozen of a Sunday, the air is gay with chim-
    ing;
In the valley full of belfries, every clapper is
    aswing;
Bell-song and bird-song, each with each is
    rhyming
In Bozen of a Sunday, when the hills are glad
    with Spring.

IN Bozen of a Sunday, between the walls of
    roses
That border merry Talfer with many-coloured
    sweet,
Children are gayer and sweeter than the posies,
And they drown the river's chatter with the
    patter of their feet.

IN BOZEN OF A SUNDAY (continued)

THE boys and girls go walking, when Ro-
sengarten's flushing.
Her eyes are on the mountain-peaks, but
little does he care
For blush of the hills, when he sees his
sweetheart blushing,
Or for sunset on the snows, when he can
see it on her hair.

THE little feet, play-weary, stumble home-
ward all around them,
For a chill steals down the valley as the
gold to silver gleams.
Shy cling their hands, as a touch unseen
had bound them,
And his eyes are full of tenderness, and hers
are full of dreams —
In Bozen of a Sunday, when the hills are
glad with Spring.

## ANNE HATHAWAY'S GARDEN

ON such a day of quiet rain
     When all the air was gray and sweet
With unseen flowers, and Spring's dear pain
Of longing in her pulses beat

SHE may have stood with arms outspread
     Among the box-trees dripping spice,
And listened for his coming tread
As for the harps of Paradise.

WE sigh for him whom God's red spur
     Drove glorious up the heights of tears,—
But in the valley, what of her,
And her long aching outgrown years?

# THE HEART OF VENICE

HERE is no song that comes unsought
  Born of a mood a breath may chill.
By labour was this beauty wrought.
Not God himself by sovereign will
Could shape this wonder like a hill
Or bid it rise like moon and sun.
Only through man such works are done.

NEED was that men should greatly do
  And greatly die, ere this could be.
The blood of glory pulses through
This golden-grounded imagery.
The very bosom of the sea
Has moulded to its ample grace
The pavement of this holy place,

As might a goddess deign to wear
The garment by her priesthood made.
The opulent shadows tame the air
That softly moves as if it prayed
Among the lives of men, portrayed
So truly, that to-day we cry —
" That is my brother — that is I."

YET not immortal — is it true
Such loveliness can disappear?
Some day will see a richer blue
Upon the sea, and through the clear
And sunlit waters, glimpses dear
Of beauty won at such a cost
It never can be wholly lost.

THE deep that gave will take again —
But this bright memory will awake
Ambition in the hearts of men
To build new beauty for the sake
Of what has vanished, and to make
Sublimer temples of the sea.
If this were immortality?

# QUEEN MARY AT FOTHERINGAY

WHAT have I gained who gave so much?
  A crown too slippery for my clutch —
A body misused and a heart abused.
What have I gained for all I spent?
Many a dead man's curse to rue,
Many a lover and not one true,
Many a bribe, though not my due —
Yet I have lived, and am content.

SAY that I squandered life — confessed.
  Had I been miser of my best,
To-day I would be in penury
Even as now, a fool betrayed.
The crown of stars and the nether flame
Both have I proved in the teeth of blame.
Have not the years in pride and shame
Given the worth of all I paid?

## QUEEN MARY AT FOTHERINGAY (cont.)

THE course I chose was the course I kept;
   In the face of doom like a flame I leapt.
Bitter and sweet have I known complete —
One adventure is left to try.
Life I have finished, mire to throne —
Here at life's end I stand alone.
Headsman, warder of worlds unknown,
Show me now what it means to die!

## LUDWIG OF BAVARIA

I HAVE been set so high above mankind
   That all alone am I.
Above me broods, ruthlessly dumb and blind,
The riddle of the sky —
The casket of the Undiscovered Light
Whose vision makes divine,
Hidden from lesser men's ignoble sight
But destined to be mine.
For I have risen to the final snow
In solitude complete,
And trodden all men live and die to know
Under my mounting feet.
Alone, alone I seek with soul afire
The sacrament supreme.
What anodyne has earth for my desire
Who famish for a dream?
Music is mine, and solitary splendour,
White, sky-encroaching peaks —
But oh, the call intolerably tender

## LUDWIG OF BAVARIA (continued)

From lips no mortal seeks,
In lands the boldest wanderer never char-
    ted,
Whose pinnacles of stone
Inviolate, whose valleys virgin-hearted
Open to me alone!
But I am weary, for the time is long;
Why does the dawn delay?
Weary of even lightning-leaps of song,
Weary of night and day,
For voices call me, call me from my sleep
So that I rest no more,
Like ripples from an undiscovered deep
Upon a lonely shore.
Bloom speedily for me, Immortal Rose,
My being to fulfil!
Haste — for the silent skies above me close
Darker . . . and darker still. . . .

## A LYNMOUTH WIDOW

HE was straight and strong, and his eyes
    were blue
As the summer meeting of sky and sea,
And the ruddy cliffs had a colder hue
Than flushed his cheek when he · married
    me.

WE passed the porch where the swallows
    breed,
We left the little brown church behind,
And I leaned on his arm, though I had no
    need,
Only to feel him so strong and kind.

ONE thing I never can quite forget;
    It grips my throat when I try to pray —
The keen salt smell of a drying net
That hung on the churchyard wall that day.

## A LYNMOUTH WIDOW (continued)

HE would have taken a long, long grave —
    A long, long grave, for he stood so
      tall . . .
    Oh God! the crash of a breaking wave,
    And the smell of the nets on the churchyard
      wall!

## THE LOVE OF WOMAN

IF he should come to me to-day
  In the strong beauty of his youth,
Profuse of hope and rich in truth,—
If he should come to me and say:
" Give me your love! Of womankind
" On you and you alone I call! "
I could but answer, " Dear and blind,
" What more is left for my bestowing?
" Without your asking or your knowing
" Have I not given all? "

AND should he come to me some day
  When withered listless leaves are blown,
Where I had waited long alone;
If he should come to me and say:
" Give me your love for charity;
" My dreams are squandered everywhere.
" My famished hopes fall dead from me
" Like the dull harvest of the air.

## THE LOVE OF WOMAN (continued)

"I seek no longer joy, but rest —
"Brief peace upon a kindly breast
"Till my tired heart is quiet clay."
I could but say, "Love, while you live,
"My love is neither mine to give
"Nor mine to take away."

# A WISH

I WOULD that we had won of love
    More than the little coin thereof,
And all the rest had flung away
The gain supreme to keep;
I would that we might understand
All that in Eden God first planned,
Ere ever men had learned to slay
Or women learned to weep.
But ah, that visions cannot last —
That perfect moments fade so fast,
And men to pettiness return
Who spoke with God erstwhile!
I would that we lay side by side
And that the curious moonbeams pried
In vain at our closed lids to learn
The secret of our smile.

## AN IDLE SONG

FREE living, free giving, may scarce be un-
    done.
  What magic recaptures the rays of the sun?
  They are fled, they are sped to the eyelids of
    men,
  And the light that is given, none taketh again.
  Sap springing, lark singing, and young hearts
    afire
  With the tender green flame of an April de-
    sire.
  It may die, it may lie like brown reeds in the
    fen,
  But the love that is given, none taketh again.

## AMORINO

WAS it a mere caprice of mateless passion?
　　So kind a memory that could never
　　　claim;
　Our little love, in quaintly childish fashion,
　Was not unworthy of the nobler name.
　Not the high god who touches the. here-
　　　after,
　Bearing within his bosom life and death,
　But a slim str　ıg Eros, winged with
　　　laughter,
　Globing bright bubble-moments with warm
　　　breath.

BEFORE the august gaze of mighty blisses
　　That since have stooped to glorify our
　　　clay,
　All unabashed, he juggles our past kisses,
　And with a smile we watch him at his play.
　He never masked in majesty forbidden,

AMORINO (continued)

Nor filched the due of greater gods than he;
Wherefore he keeps, in gentle mirth unchid-
    den,
His little share of immortality.

## SURPRISES

WHEN through the shadow thou shalt see
    Death smile
And greet him as the sleepless greet the
    light,
When thou shalt close thine eyes a little
    while
To open them in perfectness of sight,
Must not thy quickened spirit shrink for
    shame
When touched by near Omniscience to con-
    fess
How many blots of unexpected blame
Sully thy life's apparent nobleness?
But with the evil shall be manifest
Unconscious virtue that from thee hath
    sprung;
Good unpremeditated and unguessed,
Rich harvest of a seed at random flung.
That hour of vision shall to thee disclose
My love for thee, a' wild heart's thornless
    rose.

# IN DEEP PLACES

I LOVE thee, dear, and knowing mine own
      heart
With every beat I give God thanks for this;
I love thee only for the self thou art;
No wild embrace, no wisdom-shaking kiss,
No passionate pleading of a heart laid bare,
No urgent cry of love's extremity —
Strong traps to take the spirit unaware —
Not one of these I ever had of thee.
Neither of passion nor of pity wrought
Is this, the love to which at last I yield,
But shapen in the stillness of my thought
And by a birth of agony revealed.
Here is a thing to live while we do live
Which honours thee to take and me to give.

## HIS SONG FOR HER WAKING

'TIS dawn in the sky of the world,
    'Tis dawn in the sky of my heart,
And earth is the bud of a rose
Whose petals are trembling apart;
So I come to your door in the dawn
And I breathe you my life in a word.
You would smile, you would lean from
      your window, my Queen,
If you heard — if you heard.

THE earth is all throbbing with fire
    And I am a pulse of the flame;
All breathless the universe beats
Like a heart that is tuned to your name,
As the stars in their courses last night
Kept time to each breath that you drew.
But our passion is dumb — oh, my love, you
      would come
If you knew — if you knew —

HIS SONG FOR HER WAKING (continued)

YOU would glow in the flush of the dawn
 You glitter so coldly above.
You would lean like a rose to his cry
Who yearns to the lips of your love.
You would raise him who faints at your feet
To a height that his hope never dared.
You would warm the poor clod in your arms
  to a god —
If you cared — if you cared.

## THE NARROW WAY

A<sup>T</sup> sunset the young monk leaned from the wall
To greet the fisher girl who passed below.
She answered gay " Good even " to his call,
But then he sighed, " Sunset or sunrise glow
" Are both alike to me; ah, what of good
" For one so sad, holds either night or day? "

*" 'Tis twilight in the shadow of your hood —*
*" Go pray, Father — go pray! "*

"M<sup>Y</sup> soul is famished for the simple joys
" Free to mankind — why not, alas, to me?
" The throbbing outer world's insistent noise
" Allures me like a magic melody.
" With wistfulness that warms to something fonder

THE NARROW WAY (continued)

"I hear the village children at their play."

*"Their clamour could not reach the chapel yonder —*
*"Go pray, Father — go pray."*

"YOU are so sweet — Madonna's eyes are cold —

"Madonna's lips have never learned your grace.

"Ah, smile again that I may grow more bold!

"Why, hand in hand, should we not flee this place

"Of gnawing discontent and barren sorrow?"

*"Nay, Father, that's a deadly sin, they say —*
*"Beside. . . . Uguccio takes me home to-morrow!*
*"Go pray, Father — go pray."*

## THE END OF IT

THE earth weighs down my lids — they for-
    get the feeling of tears;
The heavy clods on my heart numb it to
    pleasure and pain,
And my blood shall freeze or flame to your
    mood as in bygone years
Never again, Beloved — never again.

I STROVE to see as you saw, I strove to hear
    as you heard,
I strove to stride with your strength, catch-
    ing my labouring breath,
And never you slackened your speed to toss
    me a heartening word —
Weary to death, Beloved — weary to death.

## THE END OF IT (continued)

IF you called in the name of our love, I would
    not open mine eyes;
If you called in the name of my sorrow, no
    sigh would stir in my breast;
If you called me with God's own voice, I
    would answer not nor arise,
    Now that I rest, Beloved — now that I rest.

# A MIRACLE

NEITHER in passion nor in play,
   But dreamily, half unaware,
We kissed as drowsy children may,
Sliding to sleep from evening prayer.
So brief, so calm, the passing touch
That meant so little — and so much.

FOR memory sees the wondrous thing
   The moment stood too near to know.
The fragile innocence of spring
I thought had faded long ago,
Our quiet lips found blossoming yet
Like an October violet.

# THE TOYS' COMPLAINT

WE sheltered women, love-enwrapt,
  Whose every wish is gratified,
From all adversity close lapt
In tenderness and kindly pride —
We from whose path you put aside
The possibility of care,
We women shielded and supplied —
What burdens can we have to bear?

SMILING as at a child's demands
  You fill these idle days of ours;
You give us roses for our hands
And songs to sing among our flowers.
We twine you garlands of delight —
You only ask to find us fair
When weary you come home at night. . . .
Is not our burden light to bear?

W<sup>E</sup> are the garden of your ease,
And if we bloom, you **are** content.
It would but rob you of your peace
If to your loads our shoulders bent —
But ah, to see you sad and spent!
To know the pain **we** may not share!
Pity us, Masters, and relent —
This burden is **too** great **to bear.**

## THE FORFEIT

ONLY for this, dear heart, only for this
  Do I regret
The hour earth fell away, and left our kiss
A passionate star where soul and body met.
Only for this, dear heart, only for this
Would I — if it were possible — forget.
For this — that I can never see your eyes
Without remembering their transfigured
    light
That shone upon me then
As Love drew near and took us by surprise.
That I can never give to you again
The quiet-pulsing touch of friendship only,
For memory of your touch that summer
    night.
I know that you are weary, bruised and
    lonely,
Craving a comrade's tranquil tenderness —
But since to give you more I have no right,

THE FORFEIT (continued)

I needs must give you less.
Is this the inevitable tax of pain
Because our love was fettered to a lie —
That I must see you look to me in vain
And never tell you why?
Once, only once, if I might bring to you
The comfortable balm for which you plead!
Once, only once, if I might be and do
All that you need!
But slowly, surely, like a wall of stone,
Our parted lives more hopelessly to sever,
Rises this barrier — to be overthrown
Never.
Only for this, dear heart — only for this
Do I regret. . . .

## I WAS TOO PROUD

I WAS too proud to hazard all,
  Too prudent and too wise.
I would not speak till I could see
Surrender in her eyes.
So patiently I held my peace
And waited for the sign.
I heard that she was dead, to-day —
She whispered at the end, they say,
    God's name . . . and mine.

# TO A PRESSED ROSE

LOVELY faded rose!
  Had but my fortune beckoned me
    that way
Among the silver stirrings of the day
That Nature for your blossom-triumph
  chose!
Had I but seen your maiden leaves unfold
From your immaculate heart of fragrant
  gold!
I was not there; another passed — who
  knows
How many others, lovely faded rose?
    And yet, had it been I
Who came between your crimson and the
  sky,
You would have been a rose among the
  rest —
A beauty-breathing joy upon my breast,
And then — a rain of petals by the way.

TO A PRESSED ROSE (continued)

My thanks to God or man, who chose to lay
    Your glowing over-sweet
Within the cloistered calm of this retreat.
I would not have you for my wearing — no.
It had been easy to forget you, so.
Now in my memory tenderly I close
    A lovely faded rose.

## IN MEMORY OF A DUMB FRIEND

STRANGE that so small mortality should
    leave
So large an emptiness! for as we grieve
Your little life of seven happy years
Ended for us, one who could understand
Each subtle word, and answer hand with
    hand
Had hardly taken greater toll of tears.

YET why should we not mourn as for a friend?
    That name was yours; if every man would
      spend
His life as well, earth were not hard to save.
Grant that God made your heart and brain
    but small.
What more has an archangel than his all?
And all God gave to you, to us you gave.

# TO A CHILD

LOVE me, till you learn to judge me,
 With candid sweetness unreserved.
Your growing reason must begrudge me
The honour I have not deserved.
But linger not to look beyond
When once the kindly veil is torn,
And spare a heart that still is fond
The torment of your wondering scorn.

## AUNT JANE

AUNT JANE has little shiny feet
  And pretty buttons in each ear;
She has the nicest things to eat!
I like to come and visit here.
She has a dog — his name is Roy;
He's great — we have a lot of fun.
She hasn't any little boy
And so she has to borrow one.

MY cousin Roy is very plain —
  I think he never combs his hair.
I like him better than Aunt Jane —
She has the kind of clothes that tear.
Roy never gets too tired to play —
He's always jolly — anyway,
I   like   him   better . . . through   the
    day. . . .
But when he goes to sleep at night
He doesn't care for me a bit.

AUNT JANE (continued)

But I'm not scared without a light,
Because Aunt Jane comes in to sit
And hear my prayers, and tuck the spread
Around my neck, and smooth my head,—
And then I don't care how she's dressed,
I know I love Aunt Jane the best.

AUNT JANE, of course, is very old;
　　She must be twenty-three or four.
Nothing I do can make her scold,
Not even when I bang the door.
The other day it made me cry
To think how soon Aunt Jane will die.

# LIE AWAKE SONGS

### 1

OFTEN when awake I lie
    Listening to the clocks go round
Hours and hours, I wonder why
My brother sleeps so sound.

### 2

THE city is so kind to me;
    It stays awake for company —
It never sleeps at all.
Its lamps are always burning bright
From when my mother says good-night
Until the milkmen call.
The street is always full of wheels,
Horse-carriages and aut'mobiles —
The whole night long they pass,
Carrying home to marble halls

Princesses that have been to balls
In little shoes of glass.
Then there's the dog across the way —
He must be dreaming of the day
Or barking at a kitty —
And people talking as they go . . .
I often wonder do they know
That I'm awake and like them so,
Or is it just — the City?

### 3

GOD has a house three streets away,
   And every Sunday, rain or shine,
My nurse goes there her prayers to say.
She's told me of the candles fine
That burning all night long they keep
Because God never goes to sleep.
Then there's a steeple full of bells;
All through the dark the time it tells.
I like to hear it in the night
And think about those candles bright.
I wonder if God stays awake

LIE AWAKE SONGS (continued)

For kindness, like the furnace-man
Who comes before it's day, to make
Our house as pleasant as he can.
I like to watch the sky grow blue
And think perhaps the whole world through
No one's awake but just us three,—
God and the furnace-man and me.

# A POET

HIS lips have been hallowed with flame;
   By pain they are pure to repeat
The wonderful whispers of God
That speak in the hush of his soul;
Yet if we would trace where he trod
Toward the glorious lure of his goal,
In what bitter byways of shame
Are the prints of his wandering feet!

HIS eyes have the light of the stars
   Whose secrets they search unafraid.
For him the great mystery wakes
To beauty whose vision is power;
But his face is disfigured with scars
That warfare ignoble has made,
And idly his carelessness breaks
A heart like the stem of a flower.

A POET (continued)

AND yet, to far valleys forlorn
Where saints without aureole grope
To garland the altars of light
In a blindness of patience and prayer,
Like the shout of a trumpet is borne
The vision that flashed on his sight,
And they hear in their twilight of hope,
A triumph of dawn in the air.

ALL are but parts of the Whole.
He laboureth never in vain
Who chose in marred vessels of clay
To light the unquenchable spark.
The seer who fell by the way —
The steadfast, uncomforted soul —
God, who gave birth to the twain,
Is joining their hands in the dark.

# A MINOR POET

THE firefly, flickering about
    In busy brightness, near and far
Lets not his little lamp go out
Because he cannot be a star.
He only seeks, the hour he lives,
Bravely his tiny part to play,
And all his being freely gives
To make a summer evening gay.

## ONE OF MANY

SOME sing among the trumpets in the fray —
    Such breathless glory hers might never be;
Her heart and voice were all too gentle-gray
    For such high psalmody.

BUT she could croon a little child to sleep,
    And whisper in the twilight to a maid
Who felt within her heart the springtime
    leap —
    Half-joyous, half-afraid.

SHE knew no ringing war-cry for the strong;
    Her voice no latent might to action
    charmed;
But silent rallied to her soothing song
    The fallen, the disarmed.

ONE OF MANY (continued)

NOR rose nor laurel to her burial bring —
    Above her let the green sod simply close.
Some day, from that forgotten mound may
    spring
    A laurel — or a rose.

## WHOM THE GODS LOVE

GIVE me thy youth, give me thy urgent
youth;
Thy youth to me, who know not youth nor
age.
For those who serve me I have little ruth;
My flaying scourge shall be thine only wage,
And yet I call thee from the easy way
Knowing, despite thy fear, thou wilt obey.
Give me thy youth.

GIVE me thy heart, give me thy passionate
heart;
Thy heart to me, who know not love nor
hate.
Thy flesh may be a garment rent apart,
Thy soul may shiver bare and desolate,
But though the snug hearth beckon thy de-
sire,
Me thou shalt follow from the lesser fire.
Give me thy heart.

## WHOM THE GODS LOVE (continued)

GIVE me thy life, no less — thy human life;
    Thy life to me who know not death nor
      birth,
  And I will give thee hungering and strife,
  The empty praise and mockery of earth,
  And at the last I will give thee, even I,
  One boon supreme — the readiness to die.
      Give me thy life.

# THE GUEST

THOU who tarriest at my gate,
  Pass along the sunny street.
 Do faces marred as mine is, wait
 With smiles a guest to greet?

LOVE, who touched my lips with fire,
  Sadly smiling, granted me
The fulness of my fool's desire —
A scar for all to see.

PASS — thou knowest I do not dare
  From my toil mine eyes to raise
Lest I see thee standing there
As in those other days.

BALEFUL Guest, hast thou not wrought
  All thy will of evil yet?
Hast forgot thy scar, that naught
Can soothe me to forget?

THE GUEST (continued)

CHILD, lay by thy bitterness —
　　Evil would I work thee none
Rather would I bid thee bless
What cannot be undone.

EYES grown soft with many a tear
　　Are not hasty to be hard,
And comfort speaks to shame and fear
Through lips my fire hath scarred.

DO not fear to lift thine eyes,
　　Do not fear to ope thy door.
Thou shalt know my Paradise
Who knewest my Hell of yore.

'TIS the narrow hearts that break
　　And in breaking stand confessed
Happier so, if thus they make
The Greater Love their guest.

## THE VOICE OF THE UNBORN

FROM the Unseen I come to you to-night,
    The Hope and Expectation of your world.
I am Omniscience that seeks of you
A tongue to utter the eternal thought.
I am Omnipotence that claims of you
The tools whereby my power may profit
    earth.
All Love am I, that seeks to spend itself
Embodied in a human sacrament,
For I have heard the wailing of the world,
Not faint and far away as in a dream,
But very near — and lo, I understood
It need not be.  Wherefore I come to you.

O YOU to whom my tenderness goes out,
    To whom I fain would bring an end of
      groans
    And blind, bewildered tears, a cloudless
      dawn

## THE VOICE OF THE UNBORN (continued)

Of unimagined joy and strength unguessed,
What welcome will you give to me, O
    World?
Since I whose dwelling is the universe
Will stoop to walls and rafters for your sake,
What is the home you have prepared for me?
O Men and Women, is it beautiful,
A place of peace, a house of harmony?
Will you be glad, who know me as I am,
To see me make my habitation there?
Since I will hamper my divinity
With weight of mortal raiment for your
    sake,
What vesture have you woven for my wear?
O Man and Woman who have fashioned it
Together, is it fine and clean and strong,
Made in such reverence of holy joy,
Of such unsullied substance, that your hearts
Leap with glad awe to see it clothing me,
The glory of whose nakedness you know?

## THE VOICE OF THE UNBORN (continued)

OH long long silence of the wakening years!
　　Thus have I called since man took shape
　　　as man;
Thus will I call till all mankind shall heed
And know me, who to-day am one with God,
And whom to-morrow shall behold, your
　　child.

*From the Unseen I come to you to-night. . . .*

# NEW LIFE

SPRING comes laughing down the valley
   All in white, from the snow
Where the winter's armies rally
     Loth to go.
Beauty white her garments shower
On the world where they pass,—
Hawthorn hedges, trees in flower,
Daisies in the grass.
Tremulous with longings dim,
Thickets by the river's rim
Have begun to dream of green.
Every tree is loud with birds.
Bourgeon, heart,— do thy part!
Raise a slender stalk of words
From a root unseen.

# THE STANDARD BEARER

SWIFTLY the shrieking fire-bird gleams
  Before his blank, bewildered face.
Close to his ear the bullet screams,
The battle swirls about his place.

ONE thought alone stands clear to him
  Whose rigid arms the Standard keep,
Before whose desperate eyes and dim
The ranks reel by as seen in sleep,

ONE longing — in the orchard lane,
  Far from this blazing blare of death,
To stand at twilight once again
And draw one deep, untroubled breath.

## THE DOUBLE CROWNING

LAVISH roses carpeted the ways for him;
    Noiseless beat his charger's feet, passing
      through the town.
Lavish banners made the walls ablaze for
      him,
Dancing like his young blue eyes beneath the
      golden crown.
From every crowded alley there surged into
      the street
A sweep of lifted faces, a wave of living foam.
Silken sleeves of maidens caressed his ar-
      moured feet;
All the bells were shouting when the king
      came home.

THE DOUBLE CROWNING (continued)

SILENT, smitten, gazed he o'er the press of
    them
  Where upon the market-place the Crucified
    looked down.
Silent, smiting, fell beyond the guess of them
The shadow of the Crown of Thorns across
    the golden crown.
Beyond the shimmering banners he saw the
    walls of stone,
Below the trampled flowers the streets that
    had run red,
And heavy fell upon him the burden of his
    throne —
Amid the sheaves of gladness the harvest of
    the dead.

## THE DOUBLE CROWNING (continued)

R UTHLESS ages took that hour their toll of
    him.
   All the joyous clamour of his people could
     not drown
   Ruthless ages crying to the soul of him,
   " Evermore the Crown of Thorns beneath
     the golden crown! "
   The heedless merry city, that trod its blos-
     somed floor,
   The rainbow of the banners, the drunken
     bells aswing,
   The brave blue eyes whose boyhood was
     gone forevermore,
   The shouting of the people — the silence of
     the king!

# BEAUTY

BLESSED be Beauty, that awaits
　　Our vision at our very gates!
There hangs above these meadows low
As richly strange an opal glow
As deepens into violet
Behind a Moorish minaret,
Or where the Sphinx outstares the years.
The little hills of Ramapo
Smile eastward full as goldenly
When fades the last supplanted star
As mighty mountains, rising far
Beyond the leagues of sapphire sea
That cradle white Algiers.

BLESSED be God who gave to me
　　A thankful heart and eyes that see,
Who set my feet in quiet ways
Amid his garden sweet with praise.
And yet — oh Father! what of them

Who may not even touch the hem
Of Beauty's robe — at the harsh urge
Of hopeless pain and poverty
Forever plying weary hands,
Forever straining weary eyes,
To whom the sun's ecstatic rise
Means one day more of toil's demands —
The lifting of the scourge?

AND yet, once more — a Beauty lies
  Beyond the gaze of any eyes,
Beyond the sunset islands far,
Above the throbbing morning-star,
And deeper than the sea is deep.
I have beheld, as one in sleep
Beholds a dream scarce understood,
Two lives defaced as failures are,
Ruins to pity and despise,
Maimed butts of fortune, best forgot.
These captives of the sordid lot
Looked in each other's faded eyes
And all their world was good.

# THE SACRIFICE

PALE lips that trembled under mine
   She brought to me.
A love less human than divine
They taught to me.
But now too fixedly they smile,—
Too ruddily —
Set, like a vampire's, to beguile
Men bloodily.

THOUGH time has graven on her brow
   No change to me,
The eyes she turns upon me now
Are strange to me.
Ah, dear lost love, what fiend has caught
The soul of you,
That in our happy days I thought
The whole of you?

## THE SACRIFICE (continued)

ALAS, 'twas I, to whom she gave
    Too royally.
She loved me from my living grave
Too loyally.
Heedless of all that might befall,
The cost to her
Unreckoning, she gave me all
That's lost to her.

SHE bears the burden of the sin
    Once bound on me.
She takes the rags to wrap her in
She found on me.
Thou God of Justice, I have lost
The way to her.
Take thou my life, and all it cost
Repay to her!

# THE LAME CHILD

HE passed along our village street;
The fame of him had gone before
And many ran on whispering feet
To mock or wonder or appeal.
I caught my child from where he lay
And stood expectant at the door.
Many the sick he healed that day,
But mine he did not heal.

HE paused before us where we stood
And looked into my boy's blue eyes —
Those eyes of tortured babyhood
Questioning life with hurt surprise.
It would have taken but a word
To make the future sweet and clear —
Many the prayers that day he heard,
But mine he did not hear.

## THE LAME CHILD (continued)

YET this he did — his head he bent
    And kissed my child upon the cheek.
He turned upon me, as he went,
Eyes that were wonderful with tears.
Silent I shrank before the deeps
Of mysteries too great to speak —
But oh, my patient son who creeps
Along his crippled years!

# GYPSY-HEART

MY grandsire was a vagabond
  Who made the Road his bride.
He left his son a wanderer's heart
And little enough beside;
And all his life my father heard
The fluting of a hidden bird
That lured him on from hedge to hedge
To walk the world so wide.

AND now he walks the worlds beyond
  And drifts on hidden seas
Undesecrated by a chart —
Blithe derelict at ease.
And sometimes when I halt at night,
In answer to my campfire's light
His own uplifts a glowing wedge
Among the Pleiades.

GYPSY-HEART (continued)

WOMEN are fair but all too fond;
  Home holds a man too fast.
I'll choose for mine a freeman's part
And sing as I go past.
No lighted windows beckon me,
The open sky my canopy.
I'll camp upon Creation's edge,
A wanderer to the last.

## THE VAGABOND GROWN OLD

SO warm the lighted windows glow
   Across the darkness and the snow —
The trodden road, the sodden road,
The road wherein I chose to go.

THE winter skies are steely gray —
   The winter stars are far away.
Light were my feet when winds were sweet,
But bitter going's mine to-day.

YET as I trudge, I needs must sing,
   For be he vagabond or king,
A man must choose what he will lose —
And I have known the road in spring.

## CHILDREN OF THE NIGHT

BLAME us not, ah, blame us not, ye folk who
    love the sun,
  Whose longings haunt the fields at noon,
    the ingleside at night;
  For we are of another blood and feel our
    pulses run
  As run the tides to meet the moon and leap
    beneath her light.

WE sit beside your hearth-stones with our
    faces to the fire,
  But our hearts within are straitened — (do
    ye ever understand?)
  For we long to turn away — yet dare not
    yield to the desire —
  Where the moonlight at the window beck-
    ons, beckons like a hand.

CHILDREN OF THE NIGHT (continued)

THE household phrases come to us as in a
tongue unknown.
We gaze at you unseeing, for our thoughts
are far away
Like scattered flakes of star-dust on the fly-
ing cloud-rack blown
Beyond the placid vision of the children of
the day.

BLAME us not, ye quiet ones who crouch be-
side the flame
And rule it as ye rule your souls, with meas-
ured, tranquil hand.
Nay, but my words are idle.   Give us neither
praise nor blame,
Only be blind forever, since ye cannot under-
stand.

## THE LITTLE PEOPLE

BECAUSE I dreamed with open eyes and
watched the stars at night,
Because I loved the forest and wandered
there alone,
The Little Faery People that mock at human
might
They set a spell upon me and chose me for
their own.

THE Little People told me of a country
strange and sweet —
Builded with words of beauty I saw its tow-
ers rise;
But I knew my mother listened for the com-
ing of my feet —
In tears the vision darkened and vanished
from mine eyes.

THE LITTLE PEOPLE (continued)

THE Little People bade me choose — to cast
    with them my lot,
Or nevermore to see them for mine own kin-
    dred's sake.
Their deep eyes yearned upon me, but I
    could heed them not.
My people were my people — what choice
    was mine to make?

MY people are my people and dear they are
    to me;
Yet sometimes comes a longing till I
    hardly dare to pray,
For that far land of wonder that I shall
    never see
And for the Little People from whom I
    turned away.

## HERE STOOD A HOUSE

HERE stood a house; we now can only guess
    From what scant lore the bare foundation
      yields
    The building's fashion, whose calm comeli-
      ness
    Complacent looked across the fruitful fields,
    This was a home — now fire has laughed
      and fled
    Leaving a wreck instead.

THIS was a home for human comfort
    raised —
    Now the shy creatures of the air and grass
    Nest in the blackened pit and start amazed
    If any human foot too near them pass.
    Merciless tranquil Nature takes again
    The land she lent to men.

HERE STOOD A HOUSE (continued)

BUT pity not this house, for while it stood
    Its walls were warm with comfort and en-
      shrined
Glad hearts that savoured life and found it
      good.
It was a temple of the quiet mind.
Its very altar's consecrated glow
Has wrought its overthrow.

HERE was no shameful torture of decay;
    The vivid end with sudden glory came.
In terrible beauty all was swept away,
Man's dearest art translated into flame.
So swift and shining may thy coming be,
Enlightening Death, to me.

# THE CRICKET IN THE PATH

SHE passed through the shadowy garden, so
    tall and so white,
  Her eyes on the stars and her face like an an-
    gel's upturned,
  And it seemed to my thought that the dusk
    round her head with the light
      Of an aureole burned.

BUT where she had trodden unseeing, I found
    on the path
  A cricket, so frail that her light foot had
    maimed it, yet strong
  To valiantly pipe, tiny hero, a faint aftermath
      Of its yesterday song.

THE CRICKET IN THE PATH (continued)

AND I whispered, " Alas, Little Brother, why
must it befall
That the passing of angels but cripples and
leaves us to die?
Poor imp of the greensward, God trumpets
me clear in thy call;
Thou art braver than I.


"THE Bright Ones of Heaven have trodden
me down as they passed;
I crawl in their footsteps a trampled and
impotent thing.
I know not the reason, nor question hence-
forth.   To the last,
While I live, I will sing."

# THREE WOMEN

## FIAMMETTA

HER speech like a tame serpent hisses;
    She glows like a flower of the south;
The bruises of yesterday's kisses
Are purple to-day on her mouth.
Time bears from her beauty no plunder
Nor kindles a soul in her eyes;
And to-morrow — what is there, I wonder,
To live when she dies?

## SYLVIA

IN the twilight was her birth
.Of a passion and a prayer;
Half of heaven, half of earth,
Kin to wildlings of the air.
Finely tuned to joy and pain,
At a breath her mind will stir;
Love may hurt his hands in vain
At the doorless heart of her.
Like an opal, fair with flaws,
Rarely blessed, darkly cursed,
She was made in scorn of laws,
Not quite human from the first.

G——

SISTER is she to woodlands deep
  And quiet-bosomed noonday skies;
To calm, encircling leagues of sea
Unfathomed in serenity.
Not over-quick to laugh or weep
Are the clear candours of her eyes.
The still, unboasting strength is hers
·That stays the immemorial hills.
Comfort and cheer her presence lays
Like footprints all along her ways;
The simplest of Love's ministers,
Unconscious what a place she fills.

# THE CHILD IN BLACK

OUT in the street the children play;
    They shout and laugh till I come by,
Then they are still and go away —
    I wonder why.

AND grown-up people's faces too —
    Until they see me, they are glad.
I wonder what it is I do
    That turns them sad.

AND father — when he looks at me
    He is sad too, and though he tries
To wink them back, I always see
    Tears in his eyes.

NOBODY looks at me the same
    Since mother went to Heaven to stay.
Do they think I am to blame
    For sending her away?

## ON A HILL-TOP

STEEP the ascent to which we laughing bent;
   Slowly we left the weary slope behind.
Now hand in hand upon the crest we stand
Amid the shouting welcome of the wind.

I TOO rejoice with its exultant voice
   That we upon this hill-top once have stood
Before we die, together, you and I,
To see our world and know that it is good.

TO find the worth of this perplexing earth
   Which yet is of our heaven the only gate;
Where life must be ere immortality
Can its transfiguration consummate.

ON A HILL-TOP (continued)

THE test we need ere spirit may succeed
 To perfect power and unimagined
 scope —
Where dreams untried must ever dreams
 abide
And hopeless is the unattempted hope.


WE who have caught the substance of our
 thought
May smile triumphant though our path-
 ways part.
You of my best forever stand possessed,
And greater for your greatness is my heart.

HENCE we shall turn more eager to discern
 The hid Shekinah of our neighbour's soul,
Stronger to dare our brief blind part to bear
In the slow silent growth of God's great
 Whole.

ON A HILL-TOP (continued)

A WORD, the flower of this uplifted hour
Shall turn the chill of time and space to
mirth;
A deed that springs from these forgotten
things
Shall link us yet across the breadth of
earth —

SHALL link us yet, although we may forget.
Our thoughts may pass, our inmost selves
endure.
Yea, life and death may come and go like
breath —
Wrought in our souls, this moment lives se-
cure.

## DAWN

GREEN bud of dawn
    That shyly in the east now dost unfold
The glowing garments of thy heart of gold,
I look to thee across the shadowy lawn
Hoary with dew.
Purged by clean slumber as a soul by death
I lift my brow to meet thy blessed breath.
All hail, thou messenger of Him who saith,
" Lo, I make all things new."

THE early breeze
    Quickens to sudden whispering all the
        trees;
The orchard yeomen in their sturdy ranks,
The slender cedars halted on the flanks
Of every hill, the copse's quivering green —
Even the height serene
Of the old hemlocks is a moment stirred
As if among their aged boughs they heard

DAWN (continued)

> The magic murmur of that master-word
> Thou daily speakst man's weariness to
>  cheer,
> O Dawn — would man but hear.

A   SIGN from Heaven long ago men sought,
      And he to whom their questionings were
>  brought
> Marvelled in sadness; how should even he
> Give signs to them who had no eyes to see?
> Dear God, how blindly do thy children trace
> This marvellous earth-manuscript of thine!
> Weary of study, we are baffled yet
> By the great lessons for our learning set,
> And clamour eagerly with lifted face
> To Heaven for a sign.

T   HERE shall no sign be given,
      For we are hedged with portents undi-
>  vined.
> God waits until the fetters of the mind
> At last be riven.
> And as we grope

DAWN (continued)

Amid the growing glory, we behold
The Dawn's recurrent miracle unfold
The heavenly word for hope.
The clouds of yesterday,
Although they smother all the blue, avail
No whit the mounting of the sun to stay,
Who like a strong young king in golden
    mail
Leaps up behind the gray.
Earth, air, and sea may rage in mortal strife
But calmly certain, over death and life
Rises the still, unconquerable Day.
And so shall Man arise
From sullen-clotted clouds of past mistake,
Sorrow and disappointment, and awake
With some indomitable dawn, to break
The seal of Paradise.

# THE HERO

THEY asked him for his story, when he came
    Battered and glorious from the floating
      hell
Where he had wrung his victory from death.
But he, the hero, had no tale to tell —
Simply he gave them answer, with a smile
That made them flinch and take a quicker
      breath —
" I only know we worked in sweat and flame
" And it was well worth while."

SO you shall stand some day, amazed and
    faint
Among the wondering angels, file on file
Of beautiful bright faces, all ablaze
With your achievement, vivid with your
    praise,
Asking of you, their bleeding warrior-saint,
Your own triumphant tale of battle won.

THE HERO (continued)

And you, who knew not all that you had
    done,
Shall gaze bewildered on them, reeling yet
From those long years of mortal weariness.
No hope of this upheld you in the stress —
You only knew you wrought in blood and
    sweat,
And it was well worth while.

# IMMORTAL

BECAUSE your hand
    Grew tired and laid the busy brush
        aside;
Because your weary eyes forewent their
    sight,
Shall none of all the pictures you had planned
Take form and colour for the world's de-
    light —
        Because you died?


THE hope that kept
    Through patient years of uncon-
        genial toil
Your spirit's lamp sustained with sacred oil,
The dream and the desire that never slept —
Did all the wonder-world that was your art
    Stop with your heart?

IMMORTAL (continued)

A TIME so brief
　　After your long probation, to de-
　　　clare
Your hoarded visions — strangely hard it
　　seems!
Is even God so rich beyond belief
That he from his eternity could spare
　　Your waiting dreams?

H E does not waste.
　　A thought once born, forevermore
　　　must live.
Bountiful spirit, that so loved to give,
With what a high delight you now dispense
In glorious largess, without stint or haste,
　　Your opulence!

IMMORTAL (continued)

I SEE you guide
    The hand of some young painter to
        reveal
The truth you lived so many years to feel,
Your joy in his achievement doubly deep.
Your joy . . . ah, how have we the heart to
    weep
        Because you died?

# TO WALTER SCOTT

## MELROSE

HOW often has he lingered here alone
　In such a golden evensong of spring,
Making the eye-sweet melody of stone
More lovely by his words' accompanying —
Singing for very youth of heart, compelled
By the keen urge of beauty, even as now
Tweed sings along the valley, April-swelled,
While the green slopes flush slowly to the
　plow.

## ABBOTSFORD

THIS dream come true in quaintly towered
    stone,
This palace of desire's accomplishment,
Here in his thought already had he known
A sunset calm of richly earned content,
When a harsh clarion summoned him to
    fight
In sordid lists, to purge another's shame.
Harp-hearted, he rang true, and proved him
    knight
Of that high chivalry who reck not fame,
Being content to stand with shield unstained
Before God's face.  Crown with a nation's
    meed
The Bard — but here, where patient and
    constrained
He toiled, when he had hoped to soar in-
    deed,
Humbled, be still.  His victory is gained
And of earth's wordy praise there is no need.

## DRYBURGH

HERE lies his battered armour, hacked and
    scarred
  By the long conflict. Look, what fitter
    place
  To hold the garb so honourably marred!
  Green house of sleep, from which the years
    efface
  One after one, man's futile traceries,
  As one by one frail children of the pen
  Faint slowly to forgotten silences.
  Naught is immortal but the God in men.

Lightning Source UK Ltd.
Milton Keynes UK
UKHW010727050119
334991UK00012B/911/P